F.E.A.R.

Face Everything and Rise

BOB POSTON

To Charles R. "Bucky" Poston, Sr., my dad. When this book goes to print, you will be turning ninety-one years young. When I thought about the title of this book, Dad, I immediately recalled your greatest fear twenty-five years ago when you learned you had Stage III colon cancer. You made the decision to face this head-on and go into battle. You were going to beat this cancer and declare victory over it.

The day of your surgery came, and the family was huddled in the waiting room for what seemed like an eternity. It was a long surgery. When the surgeon finally emerged, he described to us that this was a very angry cancer and that he firmly believed he got it all, but that you would have some work to do as well. I watched you stay the course through all of your follow-up chemotherapy treatments, and never did I hear you complain.

Here we are twenty-five years later, and you are still with us. Thank you for facing your enemy and that fear and not giving up!

Love you, Dad.

Table of Contents

Foreword

Have you ever been in a place in life where everything is good, but you desire more?

Do you want to go deeper because you have more in your tank than the world knows?

Sometimes you find a certain level of success, and you get content with the way things are even though you are being called to a deeper level. When you have it all but still desire even something greater, when there is a purpose deeper inside of you that you have to tap into, it often requires change. And change can be uncomfortable.

To handle any kind of change, you need to get your mind, your body, and your soul right. You need to train and develop better habits. You need to protect the most precious asset you have—the one between your ears. You also need to spend time tapping into your whispers where true profound wisdom is found. You need to have a conversation with God and listen to what He is calling you to do.

When your calling becomes so deep that it becomes a conviction, that's when you have to give up what you have in order to go to the next level. That's when you have to *give up to go up.*

That might mean selling your business or changing careers. It might mean learning to live without someone you love. It might mean you have to give up some of your old beliefs or bad habits in order to get better.

Every time I've had to give up one thing to get to another level, it's been challenging and scary.

I had to give up my dream of playing in the NFL because of a serious back injury.

When I started my gym in 2000, I had to give up being comfortable in order to follow my dream.

In 2010, I gave up a book deal, walking out of the office of Rodale Press when they told me the book needed to be called something different (fortunately, they changed their mind, and *The IMPACT Body Plan* did get published).

In my twenty-five-year fitness career, I have made many shifts from re-organizations to, most recently, bringing on a business partner. That's right. I gave up being the sole owner of my gym, Fitness Quest 10, so I could spend more time doubling down on my divine purpose of speaking, writing, and proliferating IMPACT at a deeper level.

The point is that in order to grow, you have to give up whatever is holding you back in order to get where you ultimately want to go. You have to get comfortable being uncomfortable. You have to do whatever it takes.

When I talk about living a life worth telling a story about, it's not just about showing up where you are today; it's about facing your fears so you can live up to your true potential.

I am glad that Bob has decided to share "F.E.A.R." with you. I've known Bob for about 10 years. He's a man who epitomizes all the things that it takes to overcome obstacles and to ultimately be aligned with your divine purpose. Throughout this book, you will hear from some of the people I've had the opportunity to work with and coach. Each of them knows what it takes to face challenges and overcome adversity. They have all learned to give up in order to go up.

Their stories are going to help you with all of it. They will give you the confidence and courage you need to reach your maximum potential. They will remind you that you are not alone. They will encourage you to live your best life.

And in these pages, you will discover that you, too, can face everything and rise.

Get after it!

Peace and love,

Todd Durkin, MA, CSCS
Owner, Fitness Quest 10 and Todd Durkin Enterprises
Under Armour Training Team
Head Coach, Todd Durkin Mastermind Program
   and IMPACT Coaching Program
Author, **The IMPACT Body Plan**, **The WOW Book,**
   and **Get Your Mind Right**

Introduction
by Bob Poston

F.E.A.R has two meanings: "Forget Everything and Run" or "Face Everything and Rise." Which one you choose to believe is up to you. As for me, I choose the latter.

In my sixty-plus years of walking this earth, there have been plenty of times when I have been afraid. I believe most of us can relate to being afraid of failing. And as strange as it sounds, I have even been afraid of succeeding, as it just moves the opportunity to fail up to a bigger stage or audience, right? With success, the expectations from others become higher for you to continue on that path. If you lack self-confidence, you end up placing more pressure on yourself, and because you are afraid of letting others down, being embarrassed, and failing, you choose to run from the expectation and not rise to the opportunity. You have to know that failing does not equal failure; it is a learning curve. It means you took a chance at acting on an idea or even getting something done, and it just did not work on this particular attempt. So take a step back and learn from it, refocus, restructure or redefine it, and try again. Failure, on the other hand, is you refusing to attempt that something and/or even watching someone else run with your idea. Have you heard the phrase, "If you're going to fail, fail forward"? The whole meaning of that phrase is that you use that failure to find success and continue to move forward.

The stories you will be reading here are from very dear friends of mine that did exactly what failing forward means. They are sharing very real fears and failures with you, their journeys through that fear or failure, and how they either overcame them or are working through them. Whichever path they are on, they continue to move forward. My wish for you is that you can find peace, comfort, and a strategy to deal with your fear as well—in other words, Face Everything And Rise!

CHAPTER 1

A Stroke of Love

by Julie Wilcox

On January 25, 2019, I woke up excited about the weekend and started the day with my favorite Friday TD Fitness workout. I decided to make coffee and breakfast for my husband Gary to surprise him on his day off.

Gary got up in the middle of the night, which was normal for him, and went into his home office. I fell back asleep and woke up at 5:30 a.m., rested and ready to get the day going. As I was making breakfast, I suddenly thought how strange it was that Gary hadn't come in for his cup of coffee. As I turned to the office door, I felt something settle in the pit of my stomach. My biggest fear was about to come true.

The lights were out with the door opened a crack, and I wondered, "Did he fall back asleep?" If so, that was unusual because my early riser normally got up at 4:00 a.m. As I pushed the door open, there was my Gary lying on the floor on his back, his glasses on, and his eyes wide open. I knew he was in trouble. I knelt down to check his eyes and to reassure him. "Honey, I'm here, and I'm calling for help."

His bright blues eyes smiled up at me with love and hope, which gave me the strength to act fast to get help. I called 911, my neighbor Shannon Gorrill, and woke up another neighbor, Connie Curran, by banging on her door and ringing her doorbell until her dog woke up. Trying not to panic, I could feel my heart pounding and bursting out of my chest. I kept saying to myself, "Just get here. Please, someone just get here to help Gary." When I was on the phone with 911, we did some basic testing of Gary's right and left sides. His left side was not responsive, and at that point, I knew Gary had suffered a stroke.

The paramedics were there within five minutes, but it seemed like twenty. I kept it together and stayed calm so I would not miss a thing. I knew I needed to be strong and not miss a beat. Then they took control.

The big question was how long Gary had been lying there. The answer to this question was vital to determine if he was a candidate to receive tPA, which can reduce the severity of a stroke and reverse some of the damage. Unfortunately, we didn't know the answer to that question, so he was not able to receive tPA.

I gathered a few important things, like Gary's wallet and medical folder, and climbed into the front seat of the ambulance. Feeling numb, I remember calling Todd, my boss, and saying, "I won't be coming in. I'm pretty sure Gary had a stroke." All I could do as we drove to the hospital was pray for Gary to hang on and stay with me. I was fighting for Gary's life!

We rushed Gary to Sharp Memorial in San Diego, one of the top stroke hospitals in Southern California. The ER doctors were wonderful and assessed Gary before an MRI. It confirmed that Gary suffered a massive stroke due to a blocked right carotid artery. I was given three options: Do nothing in the hopes that the clot would disappear on its own; administer the reverse drug, which was not a good option due to the high risk, which could cause a symptomatic intracranial hemorrhage; or perform a *thrombectomy* to remove the clot from an artery in the brain. Unfortunately, this procedure can cause bleeding at the point of entry or can rupture or tear a vessel in the brain. Still, it was the best option, and it was the one I chose. At that moment in my journey with God, I leaned hard on Him and prayed, "Please, God, just get him through this. He is strong. He is healthy. I know he can make it." My prayers were answered, and he survived the procedure, but the doctors nicked a blood vessel, and Gary suffered bleeding on the brain. Now we waited.

Holding God close in my heart, I began to pray again that the brain bleed would decline and the swelling subside. After several days in the ICU, we began to see progress. The bleed stayed the same, allowing Gary to move his left foot slightly. With a right-side blockage, the effects are on the left side, reducing mobility and speech. The stroke Gary experienced affected his left side, slurring his speech, causing his face to droop, and paralyzing his left arm and left leg. Basically, his brain did not recognize his left side. I kept telling myself: One day at a time, one fight at a time, and we will get through this with God by our side.

Gary kept asking for his father, who had passed in 2002, and his sister Barb, who had died in a tragic traffic accident back in 2001. That scared me so much. I thought he was seeing them and wanting to go with them. I kept praying and asking God to keep Gary with me. I wasn't ready to let him go just yet. I also asked Gary to fight and stay with me. "I need you here with me, Gary. Please stay. We have so much more to do together, and I love you more now than ever."

Ten days later, we transported Gary to a nursing rehab facility for his next phase, as he was not strong enough to endure acute rehab. This was our best option for an optimal recovery. Upon arrival, all I could do was pray that he would survive this place. It enjoyed a good reputation for rehabilitation but lacked in appearance and commitment to personal care. We were in for another sort of fight.

Someone gave me **A Stroke of Insight** by Jill Bolte Taylor, a book that changed me, the way I approached his care, and the way I worked with his team. It gave me hope. I spent hours every day committed to his care and helping Gary recover. I did not miss a PT or OT session. I knew what Gary was capable of, and I needed to be his voice and advocate if he was not only going to survive but to thrive.

On February 14, 2019, Valentine's Day also marked the anniversary of Gary's dad's death seventeen years earlier. Gary was struggling. His BP was very low, and he was as white as a ghost. We rushed Gary to the hospital to rule out another stroke. In the ambulance, Gary started to code, leaving him in serious trouble. At the hospital, I wasn't allowed to see him until he was stabilized. "God, please, I need you. I know he can pull through this."

After an hour of prayer and agony, I was able to see Gary. He was in acute kidney failure. Before his stroke, Gary weighed 165 pounds; now he was down to 140. In rehab, Gary had been on a thick liquid diet because he could not swallow properly. He hated it! He was not thriving on this diet. I promised Gary's doctor I would help Gary with two meals a day to monitor and help him start eating soft foods. He warned me that if Gary did not start eating and hydrating, he would die.

Five days later, Gary was strong enough to return to nursing rehab, but I knew that my mission was to get Gary strong enough for acute rehab. Otherwise, he would not survive.

Gary fought every day to gain strength and eat more with my help. I ate breakfast and dinner with Gary, making his juices and bringing in foods I knew he would eat. Slowly he made progress, began walking with assistance, talking more clearly, and gaining strength every day. He became the hardest-working guy in the room! We were on a mission, with God's help, to get Gary to acute rehab.

Eventually, the time came to evaluate Gary's progress. I was sure he would qualify for acute care. Gary's doctor, along with the care coordinator, informed me that Gary was not accepted. My jaw dropped, and tears welled up in my eyes.

I refused to go down without a fight. I grilled Gary's PT and OT, "Do you believe Gary can make it in Acute Rehab?" They answered me without a doubt, "Yes, Gary is strong. He has the will to get better, and he has you!" I called the care coordinator to ask why they were denying Gary the chance to get better. His answer was simple: "We don't believe he can sustain four hours of hard work a day, and if he can't make it, they won't give him another chance." I promised him Gary was ready and could do it. I laid everything on the line. How could a doctor decide who didn't know my hard-working husband? Instead, this doctor judged off notes from speech and cognitive therapists. I begged him to reconsider. I needed someone to fight for us!

With prayer and God in my heart, we got the call within twenty-four hours that Gary was accepted to Sharp Acute Rehab in San Diego. Hallelujah! My prayers were answered! For the next month, Gary had ninety minutes of PT, ninety minutes of OT, and one hour of speech therapy every day in a clean facility with a private room and private bath. I had a roll-out couch, and we enjoyed twenty-four-hour care. He saw his doctor every day, chose his own meals, and thrived on the wonderful attention.

On April 4, 2019, my sweet Gary came home! After sixty-nine days and many sleepless nights alone, I was exhausted. All I wanted was to lie in bed and cuddle, and so for two days, we did just that. We laughed, cried, held each other, watched movies, and got to know each other all over again. Our journey over those sixty-nine days laid the foundation to fall in love for the second time. It's like we were kids again—open, honest, fearless, hearts full, with a mutual respect that contained no judgment of what was to come. I asked Gary to fight, and he did. He never gave up, no matter how hard it was. That was the man I married over thirty-one years ago—determined, strong, loving, and my life partner!

Today we still fight every day to get better, one percent every day!

Here is my advice, born of prayer and perseverance:

1. **Never give up! Take it one moment at a time and live your race.**

2. Care for the caregivers. Help them to see your loved one through your eyes.

3. Fight to get better every day.

4. Keep your sense of humor.

5. Read *A Stroke of Insight* by Jill Bolte Taylor – A gift from Todd and Melanie Durkin, this book changed my life!

> *"The tragedy of life is not death*
> *but what we let die inside of us while we live."*
> —Norman Cousins

Special Acknowledgements

- Prayer time and God never leaving my side

- Family and friends

- My work family and my job

- All of the loving text messages with support and prayers

- My sister, who is my number one supporter! She helped me stay in the moment—to resist judging or predicting the future—by her unconditional love.

- My best friend, Christy, for supporting and cheerleading while her husband, Kevin (Gary's best friend and old business partner), passed away after a five-month battle with glioblastoma, a very aggressive brain cancer. We are so grateful that Kevin was able to see Gary before he passed away. One friend lost his brainpower, and the other gained a new part of his brain. Kevin will forever be in our hearts!

- Todd, Melanie, and the kids—WOW! Talk about support! Many hospital visits, calls, text messages, love, and prayers. Todd took on many of my responsibilities and rallied the team for support.

- Tom and Shannon—everyday angels!

- Jeff Bristol poured into Gary, and they have become very close. Jeff visited Gary every week after he got out of intensive care and has been training him weekly ever since.

- Caring Bridge—My sister Anni set up the Caring Bridge and helped me log updates so our family and friends would be connected on Gary's progress. Gary's college football buddies and friends poured in with great support and encouragement! This was a great way to stay connected with family and loved ones during crisis and illness.

About Julie Wilcox

Julie Wilcox is the Director of Global Development for Todd Durkin Enterprises, and prior to taking on this role in 2019, she was the GM at Fitness Quest 10 for thirteen years. Julie now helps oversee the many aspects of Todd Durkin Enterprises, including the Durkin IMPACT Podcast Show, The Todd Durkin Mastermind, and Corporate Speaking opportunities. She lives in San Diego, California, with her husband, Gary.

CHAPTER 2

Stepping Stones
by Abby Malmstrom

In August 2011, I took a leap into the unknown to become a military spouse. I decided to leave the life and business I had been building in California to adopt a lifestyle of uncertainty, deployments, and unstable career moves. Raised to be a strong, independent woman, I learned never to rely on anyone else's job for my financial freedom. Marrying into the military went against all of that, or so I thought.

On August 6th, 2011, I called home to Connecticut to share the big news with my parents. That phone call would change my life forever.

When I called home, my father didn't answer, but one of his friends did. I thought nothing of it when he said that everyone was busy and that they'd get back to me. An hour later, my phone rang. It was my older sister. She told me to sit down (never a good sign) and gave me the heartbreaking news: My father had been killed in a car accident on his way home from work, only ninety minutes earlier.

I would never get to tell my dad that I was moving. I would never get to tell my dad that I was getting married. I would never get to tell him anything. Ever. Again.

As I sat on the couch that night crying over my loss, I worried about everyone else. I felt sorry that I wasn't there to give my mom a hug. I was concerned about my (future) husband, who was already living in Mississippi, because he felt helpless that I had to navigate this loss alone. I even thought, "My personal training clients will be so disappointed that our hike in Lake Tahoe is canceled!"

Through all the thinking, reflecting, and soul searching I did that night and for the weeks and months after, it was my dad's passing that convinced me I was making the right decision to leave California, my business, and my life behind. Life was too short, and I needed to be near my would-be husband and closer to my family.

What would happen to my business? I didn't know, but soon after losing my dad, possibly even that same night, a tiny flicker of fearlessness grew inside me. What's the worst thing that could happen if I went for it? Unless my life was in danger, pursuing my new life as a military spouse *and* fitness entrepreneur couldn't be that bad. Time to face my fears and rise up to the challenges, focusing on all that could go right instead of all that could go wrong.

Even so, fear crept in again. How could I keep my business going and remain financially independent? Personal training was supposed to be, well, personal! If I wasn't there to train my clients, how could I make money?

I didn't have all the answers, but I made my decision to move. Once I committed to that choice, like magic, an idea bubbled up: What if I were to continue training my current clients even after I moved across the country? What if I offered them a way to keep me in their back pockets?

Back in 2011, the world of online fitness did not exist, nor did virtual training. What did exist was, in my opinion, useless. Zoom, Google Docs, and other file-sharing software programs were not widely used (at least for a twenty-seven-year-old fitness instructor with zero tech knowledge and zero budget). There was no FaceTime or iPhones either (in my hand, at least). I didn't even own a video camera!

However, as soon as the idea to be in their back pockets bubbled up, a series of stepping stones appeared to help get me closer to this vision. I started stepping.

My first stepping stone appeared in the form of previous knowledge. Back in college, I had taken a computer HTML language course and built my own website from scratch. That knowledge helped me put together a raw, basic web page that my clients could "log in" to. Anyone could have accessed it, but I didn't have the know-how to password protect things. I knew just enough coding to get the venture started.

All my years of hard work, personal training, and relationship building was my second stepping stone. It helped to immediately get the ball rolling. I had a list of core clients who wanted to continue training virtually with me, and they gave me the entire reason to keep pursuing this goal.

When I began to see my vision as a real possibility instead of just a dream, I checked to see if the domain www.trainerinyourbackpocket.com was available. Yes, it was! I snatched it up.

I mentioned my burgeoning idea to a client, and he loaned me his video camera. I had one week to film 200 exercises before I was scheduled to move to Mississippi. The timeline was tight. It had to happen fast. I filmed from night to the early morning at a local fitness studio.

Once I arrived in Mississippi, my vision became real. I had zero clients to work with in person, so making "Trainer in Your Back Pocket" successful online was now my only option.

Before the move, I feared becoming a military spouse because I was convinced that military life would kill my career. If it takes three years of hard work and hustle to build a personal training clientele in a new location, and we moved every three years, what would be the point of even trying? Sure, I could have a *job* as a trainer wherever we moved, but I would always be starting at the bottom of the networking mountain, even with decades of experience and a master's degree. That first year in Mississippi, I deeply resented giving up my dream of opening an in-person fitness studio in California.

But I failed to consider the flip side of fear and resentment. Moving every three to four years would benefit my virtual business now that I was able to reach untapped populations. I would train them in person, build relationships, and then transition them into my online training program. For once, being a military spouse and moving every few years had an advantage in building a business!

Four years later, when we got military orders to move from Mississippi back to California, many of my Mississippian clients wanted to continue working with me. Because I had built up the foundation for the "Trainer in Your Back Pocket" program, I had something to offer them. With one move, my virtual business numbers doubled! Maybe I was onto something. Those stepping stones brought me to an unimagined place. Now, I knew that each move with the military would afford me the opportunity to grow my online training business, rather than the dreaded thought of having to start over again.

It hasn't been easy. In fact, I've had to be pretty freakin' fearless!

On days when I have doubts or think it's not enough, that I'm not helping enough people, or that there is now too much competition in the market, I reflect on how it all began. I think back to that life-changing phone call. I think back to how my dad's death taught me that life is too short. I think back to my dream and my vision, and how I would feel if I didn't continue pursuing it. And I keep going.

I still fear that my hard work will never be fruitful or that "Trainer in Your Back Pocket" will never make enough money. I fear not helping more people achieve their full physical potential. I fear building a business alone as a solopreneur. I fear not reaching the level of success I envision for myself. But I choose to do it anyway.

What I have learned is that the flip side of our fears is powerful and life-changing, and my experience has given me some fear-fighting rules that I've come to trust.

Rule #1: Follow your intuition.

When opportunities arise, it's important to see them as stepping stones, even if you don't know what or where the next stone leads. We can't see all the stones at once. Since we don't know which opportunities will be potential stepping stones, it's important to pay attention to our intuition. The scary gut feeling that tells us to do something is a more powerful messenger than the fear that tells us to stay in our comfort zone.

Rule #2: What's the worst thing that could happen?

Ask yourself two questions: What's the worst thing that could happen if I take this risk? And what's the worst thing that could happen if I don't? When I put these questions to the test anytime I struggle to make a decision, it helps alter my perspective. It's a game-changer. For example, when I was deciding whether or not to move to Mississippi, I had many conversations with myself about the worst-case scenarios. If I moved into this new life, the worst-case scenario in my mind was that it wouldn't work out, and I would be forced to move back home, penniless and divorced. On the flip side, if I didn't take the risk of moving, I would be living with FOMO (fear of missing out) for the rest of my life. Losing the person I loved the most because of not taking the risk seemed much riskier.

Rule #3: Life can be taken away in an instant.

As I learned from my father's sudden and unexpected death, we can't take anything for granted. We can't keep waiting for things to happen *to* us. We must make things happen *for* us. While no one should live in fear of death, we are all human and must confront death. This knowledge helps remind me every day to take risks. At least I am here, still breathing on this earth and contemplating every opportunity.

Rule #4: Luck favors those who are prepared.

Take the classes. Learn the skills. Get your body in the right condition to handle what comes your way. If you are not physically able to realize your vision, then life may not give you the opportunities to make it happen. Daily physical activity along with at least one day of vigorous cardiovascular exercise and one day of total body strength training is ideal each week. Eating a diet full of organic vegetables, healthy fats, and grass-fed meats while reducing processed foods, sugar, and alcohol will play a major role in your ability to perform your daily tasks at the optimal level. Getting six to nine hours of sleep each night and resting when you're tired allows the body to recover on a daily basis. Preparing the mind to handle and cope with daily stressors and decisions through meditation, journaling, or other forms of self-renewal is essential.

Rule #5: Fear favors comfort.

Fear keeps us comfortable. Fear prevents us from branching out to try new things. It keeps us in a safe box with little risk but also little reward. Fear could have stopped me from continuing to build "Trainer in Your Back Pocket." I battled thoughts like "maybe I should just stay comfortable, rely on my husband's career, and save my time and energy from the hard work and heartache of trying to build a business." Now that I understand that our fears are simply trying to keep us safe and comfortable, I can look at them through a different lens. Do I want to stay safe, or do I want to choose to keep pushing back on my fears every day, even if it means getting uncomfortable?

If I hadn't decided to take the leap and move to Mississippi, "Trainer in Your Back Pocket" would never have been born. I'm grateful I had the guts and grit to conquer my fears, take the chance, and continue down the road to building my dream business. Even in loss, opportunities are everywhere. Just start moving forward, and you will uncover the stepping stones.

About Abby Malmstrom

With two decades of experience in the fitness industry, Abby Malmstrom is a highly trained exercise physiologist and functional nutrition coach. Abby holds a master's degree in Exercise Science with post-graduate studies in clinical nutrition. She is the creator of the 5 Weeks to 5k Running Clinic and the Trainer in Your Back Pocket® online group coaching program. Each of Abby's programs is designed to empower women with the blueprint needed to build and live in a healthy, vibrant body, all without needing a gym membership.

Blending her passion for travel with health, fitness, and empowerment, Abby hosts adventurous wellness retreats for her Trainer in Your Back Pocket® members each year. Her wellness retreats are opportunities to grow on a personal level, step outside of comfort zones, and experience the importance of building a healthy body, mind, and soul throughout the year.

When she's not busy coaching or leading wellness retreats, Abby spends her time with her beautiful daughter, McKinley, and her husband, Justin. She stays active through her favorite forms of exercise, which are hiking, running, and stand-up paddle boarding. She teaches her clients that building a strong foundation through their indoor (or in-home) workouts will help them continue living their own adventures, no matter their age.

Abby Malmstrom, MS. Owner, Trainer In Your Back Pocket® www.trainerinyourbackpocket.com

IG: @trainerinyourbackpocket

FB: @thetrainerinyourbackpocket

CHAPTER 3

Overcoming the What-Ifs and Comparing Myself to Others
By Adam Clark

Have you ever compared yourself to a friend, family member, someone in your industry, or on social media?

Of course you have. We all compare ourselves to others.

Unfortunately, this kind of comparison can become obsessive. In fact, a new form of OCD, Obsessive Compulsive Disorder, is emerging, known as Obsessive Comparison Syndrome.

My journey to become a personal trainer and studio owner—and to live as someone who wants to help change lives—hasn't been easy as I have battled Obsessive Comparison Syndrome.

The new OCD makes me shy away from engaging on social media and even in my professional life because of the what-ifs.

What if people didn't care what I had to say?

What if what I do isn't good enough?

What if people disagree with me?

What if my work isn't as good as the trainer down the street or the trainer online?

The what-ifs made me feel like an imposter and doubt my abilities. I created an invisible wall to hide myself.

But what if we flip the script?

What if people did care what I say and it could help them change their life?

What if it is good enough and it's what someone needs to take action?

What if some people disagree with me, but my message helped others get through the day?

What if people want to hear it from me and not from the trainer down the street or an online persona?

If I were ever going to own my business and establish myself as an authority in my area, I needed to tear down that invisible wall. It all started by making one post, one small step. Every great thing begins that way.

I quickly discerned that people want to hear my thoughts and enjoy my workout videos and Q&As.

They relate to me, ask questions, and I don't feel embarrassed or inadequate.

In two years, we've built Adam Clark Fitness into the strongest and most supportive fitness community in our area. We have helped people lose weight, become stronger, and break down personal barriers. We are expanding our studio. We have grown in size during a pandemic. I have written a book and presented at a national conference.

I needed the courage to overcome that fear of what-if to stop comparing myself to others with more followers on social media.

What caused that breakthrough?

I turned into a *giver*.

I had to stop being selfish and caring about what everyone would think about me.

I had to stop receiving and start giving. We are all on the receiving end in our lives, but the receiving should not outweigh the giving.

I had to start serving others and shift my mindset.

The best leaders in the world serve others and make people around them better. They give their gifts to the world. That's where I was lacking—all because I had put up this invisible wall.

This idea of turning into a giver took time. It didn't happen overnight. There were times where I said I was going to start but then shied away. If you've ever attempted a weight loss goal, I'm sure you can relate.

To become a giver and action-taker, I needed to take the first step.

In came a simple technique from a book I read, titled **The 5 Second Rule** by Mel Robbins. This best-selling book was based around the concept of counting down from five and taking action. If you don't take action within those five seconds and physically move, your brain will kill the idea.

The technique of a five-second count helped me break through, and I continue to use it today. (*Speaking of that, if you have trouble getting up in the morning, countdown from five and rip the covers off. That will get you up in a hurry!*)

Are there still challenges today? Absolutely.

Social media helps drive business, but it also has its downsides and can trip us up.

It is a time drain for most people, especially for sixteen-to-twenty-four-year-olds who average over two hours per day on it.

The more time we spend on social media, the more we compare ourselves to others. It's a trap! We fall for the beautiful beach photos, the seven-figure earner who works from a penthouse condo, people with Zeus-like abs, and the perfect love stories found on social media. Spend enough time on there, and you will start to question yourself, compare yourself unfavorably, and obsess over these people—and is what you see even real?

The truth is that social media rarely tells the true story. People post the "filtered" version of their lives.

So how do you overcome this?

I am sharing with you ten ways that helped me overcome my fear and obstacles:

1. **Cut back on social media.** More time spent on social media means less time spent on yourself. Stop trying to live someone else's life and live your own. I understand social media is a powerful medium for some, especially business owners. Start by setting a rule about how much time you want to spend on social media and put it in your daily calendar. Removing push notifications on your phone will keep you from the constant distraction. I guarantee these small shifts will be game-changers for you.

2. **What's your favorite quote?** Do you have a motto that you live by? If not, time to find one. At Adam Clark

Fitness, ours is "Get one percent better every day."
Seek continuous improvement and keep working to be
a better person. If you get a little bit better each day,
imagine what you can do in a year's time. Find that
quote or motto that resonates with you and live up to it
every single day.

3. **Find a mentor.** Every successful person has mentors.
    Don't go it alone. You don't need to speak with your
    mentor every day. You don't even need to have a
    personal relationship with this person. Someone who
    you follow online that really resonates with you can be a
    mentor. Seek out people who make you better. Without
    mentors, I'd be lost, and I am so grateful to have those
    influences in my life.

4. **Journal.** I don't keep a daily journal, but I do reflect on
    a weekly basis. Without reflection, you tend to go down
    the same path that hasn't been working for some time. I
    learned a process from one of my mentors, Todd Durkin,
    called WLAGs. It's a weekly reflection that takes only
    fifteen to thirty minutes and allows me to improve by
    listing out my wins, losses, AHA moments, and goals. I
    strongly recommend putting your thoughts on paper, so
    take some time and do it.

5. **Regular exercise.** Have you ever noticed how you feel
    after working out? Amazing, right? Exercise not only
    helps you physically, but the mental benefits are endless.

Exercise should be mandatory for everyone because it would solve many of the world's problems. Could that be the platform that I run for office someday? Maybe! Exercise comes in so many forms, and everyone can find something to enjoy. Go walking or running, hike, ride your bike, lift weights, play tennis, swim, or ski. The list goes on and on.

6. **Get rid of energy vampires.** Energy vampires are negative people who bring you down. By simply walking into a room, they drain the energy. They mope around, complain about everything, never smile, and push everyone away. Best-selling author and positivity expert Jon Gordon coined "energy vampire" in **The Energy Bus**. If you want to live your best life, you don't live it hanging around people who bring you down.

7. **Stop watching the news.** Speaking of negativity, have you ever noticed news story after news story has a negative tone? Negative news sells. The national nightly newscast always showcases the problems in the world but rarely airs stories about the good in the world. Do you know people who watch the news 24/7? They likely view the world with extreme pessimism. Why wouldn't they, when all they hear about are problems? Take five minutes to get a news update, and that's plenty.

8. **Daily personal development.** To reach your full potential, you must invest in yourself by taking time in

your daily schedule for personal development, even if it's for ten minutes. This is a must-do. In the information age, we have an abundance of podcasts, books, online courses, and videos, and most are free. Don't have ten minutes? That brings me to my next point.

9. **Learn to prioritize.** How do you think the world's most successful people accomplish so much? They prioritize. Where do you prioritize? Are you wasting time watching TV and scrolling social media? If you have big goals for your life, which you absolutely should have and are capable of accomplishing, you need to recognize what is truly important. Where do you want to be in ten years? Maybe you want to climb the corporate ladder, feel healthy and confident, and have a happy family. If so, what are you going to prioritize each day to make that happen?

10. **Sleep more.** "I'll sleep when I'm dead." I hear this a lot, but if you have this attitude, you might be living an unhealthy life. The National Sleep Foundation recommends between seven and nine hours of sleep per night. Not getting enough sleep affects your memory and alertness, compromises your immune system, dampens your mood, and decreases your productivity. Sleep is vital to your health, and if you aren't getting enough, why aren't you? Are you scrolling through social media while you lay in bed? Put the devices away and make sleep a priority. Each time you get a good night's

sleep, repeat what you did the night before and make it a habit. And if you stick with the "I'll sleep when I'm dead" motto, chances are you'll be "sleeping" sooner than if you had made it a priority.

I guarantee that if you implement these suggestions in your life, you will exponentially improve your life. You will become physically and mentally stronger. You will become more confident in yourself; you will overcome the what-ifs and the comparison game. Real lasting change starts with one action, so don't try to make too many changes all at once.

I know as a personal trainer that those who achieve the best results start by making one change at a time. They keep things simple.

Have you ever had a failed New Year's resolution?

Of course, you have. In fact, ninety-two percent of people fail to achieve New Year's resolutions because they try to change too much at once and become overwhelmed.

I achieved success one step at a time.

Looking back, it seems silly that I would care about what other people think or allow "negative head trash" to creep in and paralyze me when it came to posting on social media.

What if I had allowed that wall to stay up?

I wouldn't be where I am today, thriving and full of hope. I'd still be living in my limited comfort zone, going through the motions each day.

Where are you holding back?

How often do you put up the what-if wall?

One small step, however "insurmountable," will take down that wall!

Has comparing yourself to others kept you from becoming healthier, improving your relationships, or elevating your career?

To accomplish anything, you have to take action. Sitting on the sidelines and you will never reach your full potential.

The great U.S. president Theodore Roosevelt once said, "Comparison is the thief of joy."

You deserve to live a happy, healthy life.

Start by taking action and living life on your own terms.

About Adam Clark

Adam Clark is an accomplished personal trainer, fitness studio owner, and author.

A graduate of the University of Maine, Adam has degrees in both journalism and exercise science and combines his passion for writing and fitness to help transform lives. He published his first book, "Play Like A Champion Every Day: Your Guide to Being Your Best You." Adam owns and operates Adam Clark Fitness, a personal training studio, in Brewer, Maine, where he and his team work with many different clients to help them live their best lives.

In his spare time, he likes spending time with his wife and two cats, running, spending time at the lake, watching sports, and eating pepperoni pizza and vanilla ice cream!

CHAPTER 4

Be Afraid and Do It Anyway

by Tasha Schaded

...but those who hope in the Lord will renew their strength. They will soar on wings like eagles; they will run and not grow weary, they will walk and not be faint. — Isaiah 40:31

Would it be fair to say we all suffer from fear and face adversity to some degree? It doesn't matter if you're young or old. I have had many opportunities to overcome fear and adversity in my life. Some people choose to let it shut them down and never fight to get up, and others you can't keep down.

I always get back up and move forward. It is like working out. If it were easy, everyone would do it and do it well. It's difficult and challenging. Without the challenge, we would never get stronger. When you lift weights, eventually, the body adapts to the challenge and becomes stronger. Therefore, you must increase the challenge of the weights to grow or see change.

43

It's the same thing in life. If you increase the weight with only one muscle group, you will become overdeveloped and create imbalances in areas. Constantly change up workouts and exercises to develop strength and balance. Our minds, bodies, and spirits will grow tired when we're facing challenges alone, but our God is faithful to give us strength and stamina to keep going and keep changing.

Don't fear, for I have redeemed you; I have called you by name; you are Mine. — Isaiah 43:1

My biggest challenge is fear of failure or not being accepted. I put so much effort and heart into everything I do, but I set my expectations so high that I often don't achieve them. I didn't become a trainer until my mid-twenties. I didn't even work out before I became a trainer. A local gym owner took me under his wing, trained me, and helped me prepare to become a certified personal trainer. My amazing transformation gave me a passion for helping others have the same experience. Once I became certified, my confidence evaporated. I never felt like I knew what I was doing. I was a fraud. I had the certification, I had the transformation, I had the knowledge, but where was the confidence? Why was I so afraid of failing? What was the worst that could happen?

In my career, I have allowed people to dictate my happiness and success. I remember working for a new gym. I didn't have any clients, and I was slowly growing my business. One of the trainers gave me a hard time and made me feel like I didn't belong there, so I just quit. I had it in my head that she didn't like me and I wasn't welcome there. My emotions got the best of me, and I didn't communicate or look into why some comments were even made. I just kept telling myself for years that she didn't like me or want me there. Eventually, I found out that she was going through a rough time in her life and was just having a bad day. My running away from confrontation cost me years of negative self-talk and doubt. I was looking for acceptance and confidence in people instead of seeking to know my value and worth in the Lord.

The Lord will perfect that which concerns me. — Psalm 138:8

Another time, I started visiting another trainer's boot camp. I admired this trainer and enjoyed the intense workouts. I continued to go every week. One of the days, as I was setting up to work out, this trainer confronted me that he had been told I was there to steal clients for myself. I was embarrassed and upset since that was not the case, and I left that day with a heavy heart. I felt so rejected once again. I called my husband and asked him why I was having a hard time finding my place in the fitness community. He said that I must be doing something right and was destined for greatness. The enemy had a bull's-eye on me. He told me to be thankful and praise God that I was set apart, and He was going to bless me and use my hardships to help me grow.

Years later, I reconnected with that boot camp trainer and actually got to know him. I brought up the past incident, and he didn't even remember it happened. I later hired him to coach me with my training as a natural bodybuilder and ended up winning my division and becoming a pro!

I have learned more about believing in myself and facing adversity head-on since training with him. First, he had me buy a book called **The New Psycho-Cybernetics,** by Maxwell Maltz, M.D., F.I.C.S., about the psychology of the self and mastering mental training techniques to improve your self-image. I learned to envision myself as a pro during my workouts. Even though our worth and self-image should reflect what the Lord tells us, the devil fills our minds with doubt and low self-worth. This vicious cycle of negative thoughts quickly dominates your mind. Learning to confront and address those thoughts immediately deflects the adversity the enemy will continue to throw at you.

The Lord will work out his plans for my life—for your faithful love, O Lord, endures forever. Don't abandon me, for you made me. — Psalm 138:8

I recently opened my own business and faced real adversity. This is the hardest job I've ever had. I absolutely love training and helping clients grow and overcome their difficulties through exercise. I have absolutely struggled with being a business owner and having to make difficult decisions. It sounded like the best idea ever when I decided to make the leap, but the responsibilities and tasks are so overwhelming. I became like a two-year-old without a nap. Frequently I would wake up with feelings of doom and gloom and that I would never be successful. Fast forward three years into owning a business. Desperate for help, I constantly looked to buy into the next program, coaching, or business conference. I was at a conference when I first heard Todd Durkin speak. He lit a fire inside of me that made me desire more for myself. Who was this guy? I loved his coaching—a loud but encouraging style of motivating. I decided to join his mastermind program and become part of a team that encourages, inspires, and motivates me to do better. I still have doubts, struggles, fears, and insecurities, but it helps to know others are going through the same things I am. And now, we're doing it together!

I'm happy to report that despite all the hardships, adversities, and challenges that business ownership has brought, it has also brought so much hope, friendships, impacted my community, and transformed lives. The souls that come through my doors tell me we make them feel accepted, welcomed, loved, and challenged. Had I not gone through all the events that were meant to bring me down, I would have never been strong enough to climb to the top.

Peace I leave with you; my peace I give you. I do not give to you as the world gives. Do not let your hearts be troubled, and do not be afraid. — John 14:27

So no matter what you are going through, you will get through it, and you will see that God will not give you more than you can handle. We were designed to overcome obstacles and challenges. We are designed to be overcomers. Jesus overcame so much for us, and we have been equipped by his spirit with that same power—more than we allow ourselves to believe. God commands us not to fear or worry. He knows the enemy uses fear to keep us from victories. It took a long time to be able to stand tall in my industry and be proud and confident of being a trainer and business owner. I have helped so many people over the years, and I hope to be blessed enough to continue to help more! God's not through with me yet, and He's not through with you either. We're always in a state of growth and facing challenges to get there. Successful people fail and fail again before finally succeeding. Go ahead and be afraid. Just don't let that fear stop you from going for it!

About Tasha Schaded

Tasha started her journey in the health and fitness industry after struggling with her own weight issues. Having never been an athlete or had experience working out, losing weight was difficult and overwhelming. She hired a trainer, and after seeing amazing results in such a short time, she became passionate about wanting to help others achieve the same success. Tasha studied and achieved her National Academy of Sports Medicine Certification and began training in 2008. She challenged herself in 2012 to do a bodybuilding competition and went on to coach other women to reach their goals of walking across the stage.

Bodybuilding isn't for everyone, but if it's something you're thinking about doing, Tasha not only transforms your body but transforms and strengthens your mind to love and accept your best self! In 2016, Tasha won the open title, classic title, and overall title in a Musclemania Natural Figure Competition.

She's passionate about empowering all people to believe in themselves. Her studio was created to give a private, comfortable environment that anyone can come to feel safe and not judged. "My hope is you leave here feeling valued, encouraged, strong, and ready to take on the day!"

Tasha loves the Lord, is a happy wife, loves to brag on her three amazing children, sings at Church Unlimited, enjoys spending time with her friends, and traveling.

CHAPTER 5

He Gives You What You Need

by Teresa M. Schrodel

God is within her; she will not fall (Psalm 46:5). These words, carved into a block of wood, sit on my bathroom windowsill. My daughter gave it to me a couple of years ago. I look at it daily and smile. This simple yet powerful message from my daughter reminds me of what I should never allow myself to forget, for I am in unchartered territory. Again.

I am mourning the loss of someone I loved with all of my heart and soul, the woman who taught me how to love, how to be kind to others, even our enemies, the woman who held my hand through so many good times and too many bad times, the woman who taught me how to love God, how to be faithful to my Catholic faith, to pray the *Ave Maria* in Italian and English, and to never forget to thank God for the blessings He has bestowed on me as well as the trials I must endure.

The strongest woman I know is the woman who brought me into this world.

I knew this time would eventually arrive. I even tried to prepare myself for the inevitable, but I don't think anyone can ever truly prepare to lose your mother. I am not the first to endure this trial, but that doesn't bring me comfort. Although I have always empathized with others enduring this pain, I never imagined how hard it would hit me in the pit of my stomach. The fear of going through life without my mother makes me ache. However, as much as I once feared being alone, it is nothing compared to the misery of actually being alone.

My beautiful Italian mother, who always made sure I knew I was loved and not alone, passed away two months ago after falling down a flight of stairs in my childhood home—leaving me alone.

Even though I have the most amazing support system of people who care for me, I feel alone. This scares me. Humans are afraid to admit that we are afraid of anything. But I am not afraid to tell you I feel alone. Why? Because I have endured this before, and I want to share that story with you.

Over twenty-two years ago, happily married to my college sweetheart, I became the mother of a bouncing baby girl named Carmen. Her first year was the most joyous year of my life as we bonded and settled into a family of three.

Shortly after our daughter turned one, in the fall of 1999, my husband Michael began to experience back pain that we attributed to a wide range of causes: running after our daughter, a strain from a round of golf, or a pulled muscle from retrieving Christmas decorations in our basement. It would be five months and many appointments later for us to learn what we thought was a pulled muscle was actually a ten-centimeter mass lodged in his abdomen and pressing on his spinal cord. At twenty-nine years old, my husband of five years was diagnosed with testicular cancer.

Despite the horror of that period of my young life, I was never alone. While my toddler was asleep in the same room I grew up in, my brother, two years my senior, sat on the couch with my parents as we learned the news of this diagnosis. My devoted in-laws came immediately to be with us from their farm two hours away. Our families and friends never left our sides as Michael endured more than eighteen months of chemotherapy, radiation, surgery, and test after test after test. Many of these tests and treatments took place in Baltimore, but after the first six months, an oncologist in Indiana took over Michael's care, forcing us to travel back and forth to his team in Indianapolis. We left Carmen home with my parents to care for her.

I prayed every single night. I prayed the same prayers my mother and father taught me as I tucked our daughter into bed when I could be home with her. I attended Mass and begged God for the cancer to be gone and for Michael to be cured. Michael couldn't die. He was too young. I needed him. Our daughter needed her dad to teach her so many things. We were determined he would survive this battle. He simply *had* to survive.

In the end, after two months of loving care from hospice nurses, volunteers, friends, and family, God did cure Michael—not the way I was begging for, but the way God intended. Michael was at peace when he went to heaven a month after he turned thirty-one. And I was alone with a two-year-old.

I was scared. I was anxious. But I am strong. I am my mother's daughter.

After a month of commuting between my parents' and our home, ten miles apart, to feed the cat and check the mail, my aunt gave me some wise advice: I needed to live alone at our house if I had any hope of realizing the plans Michael and I had of building our dream home close to my parents. A month after becoming a widow, and two weeks after the horror of 9/11, I moved back into the home Michael and I purchased a month before we married, the same home he passed away in. And thus began my life as the lone parent.

I wasn't by myself, for I had my parents, brother, my in-laws, and many friends to help me. But I was alone.

At night, I was the only one tucking Carmen into bed. I was the only one taking care of our home. I was the only one paying bills. I was the only one in my bed at night worrying about the many things for the next day, week, month, year, as well as Carmen's health, education, and her every need. I was alone handling life. And no one was handling me.

My mother, daughter, and I became a three-generation team that worked together in the family retail business, went shopping together, to church, to the park, and on vacations. My mother never let me feel or be alone. She was always at work with me or a mile (or a phone call) away. Yet I still felt alone. So I kept myself busy by serving on hospice and chamber boards and committees. I also began to volunteer at church more and volunteered at Carmen's parochial school, where she started two weeks after her father passed away. This school is where my faith in God deepened more than I could ever have expected. The teachers and staff, both religious and lay, and parents became my lifeline, and I never felt truly alone.

Eventually, Carmen graduated and went off to college preparatory parochial high school, traveling an hour each way, which left me alone many evenings. Alone. I was alone. I was scared. I attempted to keep myself busy until I recognized I *needed* to be alone. From the moment I became a mother, I had become a caregiver. Growing up, Carmen depended on me for her every need. Now that she was in high school, she didn't need me in the same way, but she needed me more than ever. (Side note: I often tell my friends that once their children hit this age and enter high school, they should consider themselves on call more than ever. Be prepared for their desires to chat at night when you are going to sleep. They will tell you anything if you sit and listen and allow them the time to open up to you. Embrace this intrusion on your sleep as a gift from God that your child wants to be with you. Do not complain. Do not be selfish. Embrace.)

I survived her high school years and sent her off to college two hours away, and for the very first time in my life, I was physically alone. Even with my family and friends by my side, I was still alone at night. There were tears those first few days. Okay, I lied; there were tears until spring break of her first year because it took me that long to accept it was okay that she didn't need me as much. I had done a decent enough job that she was strong enough to "fly." I began to embrace the time alone to do crazy things like clean my house and start graduate school.

With my well-worn groove intact, my fear of being alone mostly melted away until two months ago when my mother passed away tragically, and once again, I felt my world pulled away from me.

My rock, the woman who always made sure I never was alone, was gone. It's a surreal feeling to lose a parent, and for a woman, losing her mother is tragic. The first of our three-generation team is gone forever. I cannot explain this feeling, but it is a pain deep inside that no one can make better. The grief of becoming a widow at twenty-nine feels like nothing compared to this, though I suspect I have blocked out the pain I endured nineteen years ago.

The thought that I lost my beautiful, kind, loving mother, whom I saw or spoke to daily for almost forty-nine years, can at times paralyze me. I am still in shock. No more phone calls before I go to bed. No more sharing of advice. No more shopping trips, vacations, or sitting beside each other in church. No more of her delicious sauce to soak up with a piece of bread. No more the security of knowing that I am not alone because my mom is always there. My "person" is gone, and I feel lost.

Grief brings with it a rollercoaster of emotions. I have a strong ninety-one-year-old father, a college senior, my brother (also in the form of my business partner), and friends who need me. I have the memories of the multitude of adventures taken with my beautiful Italian mother. Day-to-day tasks have become easier, but the final removal of her clothes from her closet and drawers still waits. I sometimes manage to fill a bag; other times, I simply sit on her bedroom floor and weep. I am not afraid to face these emotions. I am sad, but it is not a weakness. It is the reality of mourning the loss of someone you love so deeply.

Cooking has become less of a chore and more of a connection to my mother, who I often joke had the talent to make water taste amazing. I made her sauce recently, and as my daughter smelled the mixture of spices and tomatoes simmering on the stove, she smiled at me with tears in her eyes and said, "Smells just like Nonna's." Perhaps she left me a bit of her passion for cooking.

Above all, though, my mother had the strongest faith in God, and she passed that along to my brother and me. My faith lets me know I will be okay. I don't need to be afraid of being alone or not being strong or not being able to manage my life, because I have God. I am okay, and I will be okay.

God doesn't give you what you want; He gives you what you need.

God is within her; she will not fall.

About Teresa M. Schrodel

Teresa Schrodel is the Gallery Director and co-owner of Medart Gallery in Dunkirk, Maryland, an art and custom framing business founded in Italy by her parents, William and the late AnnaMaria Radosevic, in 1968. She has a passion for helping her community, and you can find her volunteering and supporting activities and fundraisers. Teresa is currently serving as a member of the Board of Directors for the Calvert County Chamber of Commerce and an ad-hoc member of the Marketing and Development Committee for Calvert Hospice, where she previously served as a member of their Board of Directors for two terms. She also served on the board of directors for the Southern Anne Arundel Chamber of Commerce.

Teresa is the widow of the late Michael D. Schrodel and mother to their daughter Carmen. In 2002, she and a fraternity brother of Michael's began hosting an annual golf tournament to reunite friends and raise money for various organizations, specifically a scholarship fund at Frostburg State University, in Frostburg, MD, where Michael and Teresa met, and Calvert Hospice in Calvert County, Maryland. Their daughter, Carmen, has taken the reins of the annual tournament, currently held in Lothian, MD. (See MDSGolfClassic.com.)

Teresa is also active in her church, Jesus the Good Shepherd Catholic Church, in Owings, MD, currently serving as a Lector in the Liturgical Ministry where she and her family are founding members. Teresa keeps herself busy with her family and friends, working out at Poston's Fitness for Life and studying for her master's in Business Administration with a focus on marketing.

CHAPTER 6

I'm Not Good Enough

by Hugo Brambila

Most of my life, I've wrestled with feeling not being good enough—in school, sports, my career, marriage, parenting, and even life. When I was growing up, my dad pushed me to be better at soccer. He always told me what I could do better but seldom offered praise to confirm that I did a good job. As he repeatedly told me how to get better, the thought that I was not good enough began to take root in my head.

Those thoughts of not being good enough were just thoughts. They were not true, but I repeated them so often in my head that I accepted them as a reality. This false belief dogged me through college and into the beginning of my career.

In 2002, as I started my collegiate soccer career, contemplating what school to attend, my club soccer coach told me I wasn't good enough to play D1 soccer. This opinion, along with injuries, drove me to choose a D2 school. The thought of not being good enough drove me to choose a path that I wasn't 100% sold on.

At training camp, the freshmen were paired up to house with the returning seniors. The night before I was to try out, I was nervous, and anxious thoughts swirled through my head: *Am I good enough to be out here? Am I going to get cut? What if I fail?*

After the first week of camp, BK, the senior I was paired up with, asked me what was wrong because I had this nervous look on my face.

"I don't know if I'm going to make it," I told him.

"Are you kidding me?" he asked.

"Yeah," I said. "I could be better."

He replied, "But you're one of the best ones out there!"

Other people could see my potential, yet I didn't think it was in me. Two years later, I became a captain on the team and helped lead us to the first-ever playoff appearance in school history.

Soccer opened up a lot of doors for me. I was fortunate to be able to play professionally. Even though only one percent of athletes make it to that level, I still doubted myself. This belief system persisted long after my athletic career, following me into my business, my marriage, and into parenting.

Many times in the past, I let others' opinions dictate what I could and couldn't do.

It wasn't until I began to surround myself with positive people and was introduced to self-discovery that I realized everything I need to be successful has always been inside of me.

As a child, I was always aware of my own gifts; I was innocent, pure, and creative. My imagination had no boundaries, and my dreams had no limits. I lived totally in the moment. As I grew up, I began to betray who I truly was, buying into the beliefs of others. I became a pleaser, thinking and acting in ways others wanted me to. Through the help of some amazing coaches and books that were recommended, I came to realize I have no obligation to succeed; I only have an obligation to be true to myself and go after my dreams. I started to dig deep into myself and found that I *love* coaching others. I began to pour my heart into coaching, showing up each day, and giving it my all. It was like going back to the days of being a child and truly enjoying every second of what I did! I came to realize what other people had to say couldn't impact me unless I let it.

Now, every day is not perfect. I do not succeed at everything I do, but I take those opportunities and struggles and try to learn. As I grow, I turn them into wins.

To this day, I continue to struggle, but I have found that these five tools help me snap out of it. When I focus on these five things, it helps me overcome my fear and thoughts of not being good enough.

1. **Talk to yourself instead of listening to yourself.**

    Often, saying what you are thinking out loud makes things much easier. When we think, we let the words get in our heads. When we say those same words out loud, we get a different perspective of things. When those thoughts of not being good enough come creeping back into your head, speak them out loud. They may sound silly, but once you do, it helps you shift your mindset.

2. **Everything you need is inside of you.**

    I once heard an old story that goes like this:

    "In the East, many thousands of years ago, it was believed that every person on Earth was a god. But humankind abused their powers, so the Lord decided that he'd take it all away. The question then became where he would hide this power, the source of all human talent, potential, and glory. The advisors said, 'Dig a hole deep in the ground,' 'Put it on the top of the highest mountain,' and 'Place it in the bottom of the deepest ocean.'

    'No,' the Lord replied, as all these places can be reached by mankind. After a few moments, the Lord spoke knowingly, 'I have a solution. I will place this source of extraordinary power and glory inside the heart of every man, woman, and child on the planet, for they'll never think to look there."

I believe we get caught up looking for things outside of us, but when we look inside or, as my mentor Todd Durkin says, "Listen to the whispers," we can find all the power in the world to accomplish what we set out to do.

3. **Guard your mind.**

   Our mind is a garden, and we cannot let weeds take it over. The mind is its own place and can make a heaven out of hell or hell out of heaven. Don't allow negativity to gather in your mind. There will be no room for happiness. Don't get caught up in the past. Never worry about tomorrow; live in the present. Stand guard at the door of your mind and make sure you create a beautiful garden.

4. **Create a highlight reel.**

   You are amazing and have done some amazing things in your life. Take some time and write down all of your accomplishments. Anytime you doubt yourself, take a look at your highlight reel and remind yourself, "You can do it!"

5. **The power of a Mastermind Group.**

   Join a group of people that supports you and challenges you to get better. I'm so thankful for the Todd Durkin

Mastermind Group. Since I've joined this group, I've elevated my thinking and actions tenfold.

6. And then some...

Have faith and take action. Only *action* gives life to strength. Have a definite purpose in life and keep reminding yourself of your goals and why you do what you do. I find that when I'm not working toward a goal, I tend to drift. Drifting leads to my mind having a chance to think, and some of those thoughts can be negative.

It's a constant battle; the thought of not being good enough still appears in my life. Now, I'm well equipped with the tools to remind myself *I am good enough*, and I am truly worthy of being the leader I am. Trust the process and take action.

About Hugo Brambila

Hugo Brambila is a performance and IMPACT coach from Sacramento, CA, and an exercise science graduate from California State University Stanislaus. He was a four-year member and two-year captain of the school's Soccer Team, leading them to their first-ever NCAA tournament appearance. In 2012 Hugo founded Custom Fitness, a personal training facility in Sacramento, CA. There, he has committed himself share his passion for fitness with athletes and non-athletes alike.

CHAPTER 7

That One Moment
by Jackie Balboni

We are all familiar with stories of how suddenly and drastically someone's life and perspective change. "Face everything and rise" isn't just a phrase for me but an actual event.

I thought I had mastered the health and wellness thing. I was a personal trainer, a kickboxing instructor, in training for my black belt in Tae Kwon Do, a mom of three beautiful daughters, and working full-time in a commercial gym. I worked out regularly with lots of cardio and considered that my salad at dinner meant I was eating a ton of vegetables. My fluids were ninety percent caffeine. I didn't get enough rest but pushed through long days trying to get everything done.

Looking back, I can see I truly didn't understand wellness and certainly didn't grasp the negative impact my lifestyle was having on my health. My work with my personal training clients often led to conversations about recent check-ups or communicating with their doctors about their state of wellness, all the while failing to follow my own advice.

I had my third daughter when I was twenty-six, and after her delivery, I was exhausted beyond what was normal for a new mom. My doctor was quick to look into other causes of my fatigue instead of attributing it to postpartum issues. I was diagnosed with hypothyroid and put on medication. While it helped a great deal, I never quite went back to feeling like myself. Life continued, and so did I, pushing myself. Then three things happened that really changed my life.

The first event was when I glanced in the mirror during my daily walk-through checking equipment and greeting members. My pale, skeletal face shocked me.

The second event occurred when a training client pointed out the goiter I had developed due to my hypothyroid condition and asked me if everything was okay. She noted that I didn't look well, and her genuine concern forced me to pay attention.

The third sign was during a routine acupuncture appointment for migraines. My acupuncturist paused and asked me when I had last been to the endocrinologist. I said, "Oh, I need to go." He abruptly stopped treating me and insisted that I "get up and go." I was shocked, but his urgency made me act. I reached out to my doctor, scheduled an appointment, and asked her to examine the goiter. I asked if it could be removed, given that I was on medication now for the rest of my life. She agreed and sent me to a surgeon who did a more thorough examination and biopsy. The goiter was pushing on my windpipe and vocal cords and had to be removed.

Those three signs motivated me to have the surgery, where they conducted an even more extensive biopsy. Afterward, I sat in the doctor's office to discuss the results. It had been two months since the goiter was removed, and I wondered why I was pushing so hard to get the results now. What else could be the problem? As I sat down with the surgeon, I vividly remember him turning his back to me as he informed me that my thyroid had been removed and that I had malignant carci—I couldn't hear any more as tears literally rushed into my eyes. I couldn't hear. I couldn't focus. I never ever expected to hear that diagnosis.

Stunned, I went and sat in my car. I think I sat there for a half hour, bombarded with thoughts and fears. I called my husband and told him what the doctor said. He asked me, "Are you gonna die?"

In that moment, that question became a "face everything and rise" moment for me. I yelled, "No, of course not!" I didn't know what to think, but somehow, I knew I had to face it and do everything in my power to be healthy. I wanted to stay with my family. I will never know what made me so certain that I was going to fight through, but I was sure, without a doubt.

For the next year, during and after radiation treatment, health and wellness took on a whole new meaning for me. Every day I battled fatigue and worry. I learned so much that year. I researched nutrition. I revamped my whole fitness mindset. I began lifting weights and getting stronger. I learned how to manage my energy! I looked at things differently.

The trainer I am now looks nothing like who I was at twenty-six. My "face everything and rise" moment has been an opportunity to challenge myself to learn new things and to help more people. Professionally, I train wellness, working out correctly, eating to thrive, prioritizing rest, and stress reduction strategies. Personally, I'm so grateful to say I survived that diagnosis, and it has only made me want to help more people take better care of themselves. I want everyone to know that they can come out the other side of any challenge stronger, wiser, and better.

About Jackie Balboni

Jackie Balboni is the owner and head trainer at Dynamic Fitness Results in South Windsor, CT. Helping adults look better, move better, and feel better is her focus! She is a mother of three daughters, a fourth-degree black belt in taekwondo, a figure competitor, a twenty-two-year veteran personal trainer, and group instructor.

CHAPTER 8

I'll Never Forget

by Susan Bonin

September 11, 2001—a day that will never be forgotten.

I had recently moved back home to Pennsylvania to deliver our first daughter, Ryan. She was six weeks premature and weighed only four pounds when she was born. Just twelve weeks later, as we awakened for breakfast, I turned on the TV to catch up on the day's news. What was unfolding on the screen was something out of a movie: airplanes crashing into the Twin Towers! I checked the channel to be sure that I was on the news network. Just then, my husband Marc came into the house from his night shift, shouting that terrorists had overtaken airline jets and were flying them into the towers and the Pentagon.

My heart began to race, and I held Ryan just a little tighter. My brother and my brother-in-law were both pilots. Were they on these flights? Would my husband and I be called to help care for the wounded? We were only two hours from the city. What would I do with the baby? She was still so small. I couldn't bear the thought of leaving her. I sat on the couch in disbelief. Suddenly, everything I was so sure of was unraveling. Terrorists on American soil? Surely there will be war.

Then our cell phones and the house phone began ringing. Our family and friends were asking all of the same questions that no one had the answers to. Everything felt out of control. I had to get control. Marc was exhausted from the night, so I sent him to rest. I unplugged the phones, fed the baby, and put her down to nap. The next few hours were spent watching the updates on TV; I couldn't pull away. That night, sleep wouldn't come. I was so riddled with anxiety that I could not turn my thoughts off. Fear had crept in and would not leave, and I would battle this fear and its many faces for a long time.

We didn't end up traveling to help. There was plenty to do in our own area. Suddenly, all hospitals and clinics were developing disaster plans and practicing intruder drills. Our lives became consumed with protection plans and new protocols. People began stockpiling dry foods and water in preparation for what might come next. Schools became designated disaster shelters. People began drawing money out of the banks. An isolated incident was changing the way we all lived and creating doubt in our safety.

After that day, I was hyper-vigilant whenever I was outside my home, especially if the baby was with me. I was constantly looking for anything that seemed out of order or for people who didn't seem to fit in. When we had to travel, I couldn't sleep for fear that our plane would crash or someone would enter our hotel room. These fears were irrational and nebulous, and I knew it, but I could not talk myself out of it no matter how hard I tried.

My husband noticed that my once carefree demeanor had been replaced this hypervigilance. I told him I was just tired from being a new mom; everything was okay. We both knew this was a lie. I would keep working on it, I told myself. It will get better. I just need time. Unfortunately, the opposite occurred. I found reasons to stay at home, asking Marc to pick things up for me on the way home from work. I had my family visit at my house instead of going to theirs. I talked about bills when my husband wanted to plan vacations. Things were just getting worse.

Winter dragged on, and life became very routine. I felt comfortable at home. We were safe there. I could finally feel myself starting to relax, comforted by my locked door. Snowfall was heavy that year, making my isolation even easier to explain away. I kept up with my family and friends on the phone and made promises to visit "when the weather was better." I filled my days with housework and caring for the baby, telling myself this was idyllic, how a new family should be. I'm certain there were many weeks in succession that I never stepped outside. Ironically, I don't remember being bothered by being inside, but I do recall many invitations I declined without a thought, preferring to stay in my nest.

Then came spring. Ryan was starting to crawl and loved to sit by the glass door to our patio. She would get so excited by birds and squirrels in the backyard. She could sit for hours in the sunlight. Marc built her a playground with a swing set outside. I remember getting angry with him. It wasn't a safe enough swing; the slide was too high; she was too small. I remember my heart racing when he took her out there anyway and the look of sheer delight she had when he started to push her on the swing. I was fully panicked, and she was exhilarated! The look on her face was pure joy. As her peals of laughter ripped through the air, I couldn't help but laugh as well. I realized that if I didn't get hold of my anxiety, if I didn't let my daughter play and explore and adventure, I would be stealing her most precious gift—life with all of its ups and downs, all of its darkness and light, life that is only available to us for a short time. Who was I to steal that from her? How could I think that the only way to protect her was to deprive her of these joys?

I had to do better. On that day, I decided that I would make a change. I started to talk out my fears with my husband. I started back to exercise to help relieve stress and clear my head. I started to take Ryan outside more and eventually began taking her shopping and visiting friends. Each time we went and nothing bad happened, I felt more confident. She was always so excited to get outside, to visit a new place, to smile at strangers. Her ease suddenly became my ease again. Astonishingly, my toddler was curing me of my anxiety.

Together, we became adventurers, taking day trips to the zoo and visiting friends and family. Soon, packing a bag and taking off for the day was a regular activity for the two of us. We created the most wonderful memories in those days, and in time, fear was replaced with excitement for what was to come.

I'm not going to say that I don't struggle with anxiety every now and then. But I will say that I meet my fears with a new perspective. Instead of being crippled in the moment, I try to look at the situation before me and assess. Is it really dangerous? What's the worst thing that could happen, and how likely is it? Is this fear so important that I should allow it to take the joy out of the situation? Nine times out of ten, the answer is no. I ignore the fear and carry on. In a weird game of rock/paper/scissors, perspective crushes fear every time and leads to the most amazing experiences.

That toddler is now nineteen. She continues to be fearless and continues to make me step out of my comfort zone as well. She may never know how she changed my life, but I will always be grateful to her. She reminded me to live fiercely, unapologetically, and without fear.

About Susan Bolick-Bonin

Susan Bolick-Bonin has been a Family Medicine and Emergency Medicine Physician Assistant for twenty-two years. Her love of medicine and fitness and affinity for helping people created a natural interest in the world of personal training. Susan is a NASM certified personal trainer, an RYT 200 yoga instructor with Yoga Alliance, practicing Vinyasa flow, and is certified to instruct Bosu, Zumba, Strong by Zumba and Pound as well as various boot camp and circuit-style group fitness classes. She is currently a personal trainer and group fitness instructor at Evolution Barbell in Myerstown, PA. Susan currently resides in Lebanon, PA, with her husband Marc and two daughters, Ryan and Lilianne.

CHAPTER 9

Voices From the Summit
by Jarod Cogswell

"Guys, we need to remain calm and come up with a quick plan. The hole of the cave is filled in, and we're going to suffocate if we don't keep our shit together."

It was 3:00 a.m. We had spent the last twenty-four hours without water, climbing a mountain through a ferocious storm to 11,000 feet in elevation in fifty mph winds and minus forty-degree wind chills and hours stopping to build what turned out to be a pathetic snow shelter near the summit of the mountain. The fear inside of me mounted to its peak.

I looked down at my feet, searching for the entry/exit hole of our snow cave, and sure enough, it was gone.

There was no way out.

I've always loved the mountains ever since I can remember—the smell of the trees, the clean, crisp air, the sounds and warmth of a good campfire. My senses have always been ignited in the mountains. Even food seems to taste better.

When I first started climbing in the Sierra Nevada, it was simply to escape the crowds at the resorts. I loved to ride my snowboard down untouched descents with a brotherhood of friends who loved what I loved. "Earnin' our turns" was our motto, and I was constantly exploring new possibilities in the backcountry. Truth is, I was addicted to the constant challenge of reaching a summit for the reward of snow surfing through fresh powder, screaming through the trees like a happy kid, then high fiving my "bros" at the bottom of the descent.

Eventually, I moved up north to Oregon. I stepped up my mountain skills, enrolled in a few avalanche courses, and spent countless hours training on rock, snow, and ice. I could see Mt. Hood from my new neighborhood, and I met my first climbing mentor, Erik Broms. One cold morning, "The Brominator" guided me up Hood for my first summit of the mountain, and of course, I was hooked as I stood on top of that 11,000-foot volcano. I could see views of Rainier, St. Helens, Mt. Adams, and so many other mountains I would eventually climb.

A couple of years later, I registered for a snow and ice course and began climbing more technical and challenging routes up Hood, a.k.a. "Wy'east" (the original name given by Native Americans who first inhabited the area). Some friends took the class with me, and we discussed climbing Leuthold Couloir that runs up the West Face of the mountain. I had never climbed the route before but had climbed the Reid Headwall route, which is very close by.

I was stoked for the challenging route and to share a rope with some accomplished climbers and friends (Jim and David had climbed in Alaska together; Keith in the Himalayas). I asked my buddy, Bob P., if he wanted to join. We had become great friends in a short time, and we both enjoyed taking our Golden Retrievers for backcountry snowboarding adventures.

As the day of the climb approached, Bob called me with concerns about the weather. Light spotty rain was forecast, but it didn't worry me. I had experience with bad weather and had now reached the summit of Hood over fifteen times. I always felt that bad weather and suffering was part of the deal.

Bob agreed, and we stuck to the original plan.

The next morning brought typical winter weather, cold and cloudy with occasional snow flurries. That January, the snow level was low in comparison to the annual averages. Regardless, the five of us began the trek at 4:00 a.m. from the south side of the mountain. The goal was to hike up to Illumination Saddle at 9,200 feet of elevation, which would take us to reach the Reid Glacier and eventually traverse to the base of the Leuthold route.

When we reached the top of the Palmer Glacier at 8,700 feet, I remember my hands getting numb from the winter cold. The temps were extreme, so I started waving my arms in a circular motion to re-gain blood flow for warmth. This sometimes happens in cold temperatures. It can be very painful and take the wind out of you, and that's exactly what happened. As one of my climbing mentors, Mark Twight, once said, "Embrace the suffering. It's what you signed up for."

When we reached the saddle, the sun started to peek out of the clouds giving me a little more confidence about how the day would unfold. From here, we roped up into two separate teams—Jim, David, and Keith on one rope with Bob and me on the other. We then started to traverse over the Reid to the base of Leuthold. Again, there wasn't a lot of snow yet for that time of year, and we spent a little bit of time navigating through crevasses. Eventually, we made it to the bottom of the route and began climbing upward.

I felt strong as I moved up the mountain. I always find the routes off the beaten path exhilarating and private. No crowds, just the boys and me attempting a new route for ourselves. Then as we reached 9,600 feet, I stopped to look around. It was spectacular! The route was steep and aesthetic, but far off in the distance, I could see some clouds coming toward us, and it was getting colder. Nonetheless, we forged on.

Soon after, we caught up to a group of three climbers from Montana. One of the guys was belaying (securing a climber from a potential fall) his partner above, and the other was tied into his anchor. They seemed to be heading down, so I asked one of them what they were up to. The climber said that they were going to abandon the route due to weather concerns, and he admitted, "I'm out of my comfort zone."

I shrugged it off and kept moving up the mountain but continued to pay attention to the clouds behind me, which seemed to be moving toward us quickly. Our other rope team was up above, and I set up a belay for Bob, who was on lead to navigate around the corner of a large snow mushroom.

At that moment, the clouds moved in and engulfed us. Visibility decreased dramatically, and the winds picked up. I put on my belay jacket and goggles and stood on belay for what seemed to be an hour or so. My hands were freezing, and the pain from the cold was relentless. I couldn't understand what was taking so long as Bob was not out of sight.

"What the F is going on up there?" I yelled out loud and tried to keep myself warm at the same time.

Finally, I felt a tug on the rope signaling me to begin climbing.

I moved fast, and the sky began shooting BB-sized pellets of ice. I put my goggles on, but for some reason, the ice froze directly to my lenses. I couldn't see, but when I took them off, my eyes and eyelids felt like they were being struck by needles of ice.

When I reached the team above, we decided to connect our two ropes to ensure we stayed together. Visibility was deteriorating, and we were up high on very steep terrain on the mountain. This was the point of no return. It was actually more dangerous to try and rappel down versus gaining the summit and descending the safer, traditional south side route.

Footing became more difficult as well as we ascended the steep slope. The snow was inconsistent, making us slip even with our crampons on (snow spikes placed on climbing boots). We were moving too slow to gain the summit before dark.

The winds began to howl. Bob was less than fifty feet from me, and we couldn't communicate by voice. We started communicating by the number of rope tugs, which worked well given that I had to stop and "clean the route" (removing snow and ice protection from the route using pickets and ice screws).

As time marched on, conditions worsened, and I worried about navigating this technical route in the dark. Suddenly, I slipped and slid down the steep slope about ten yards. Thankfully, I was belayed by Bob as he felt the rope tug behind him. It was a short fall, but my heart was racing.

By this time, I also knew that we were off of our original intended route. Although visibility was low, it looked like the

Reid Glacier Headwall route I had climbed for the first time with Jim. I really wanted to beat the darkness to the top of the summit, but it was becoming almost impossible due to our slow movement. In addition, our water and food were frozen, so we were all unable to fuel ourselves and hydrate.

About twelve hours into the climb, darkness came upon us right as we began to gain the summit ridge. With headlamps, we navigated the best we could, but the ridge was narrow and filled with heavy winds and snow, making it stressful. A fall to the south side was a 1,500-foot drop and 2,000+ to the north. At one point, as I was wrapping a picket around my shoulder, my headlamp flew off my climbing helmet. I somehow caught it! My heart pounded as there was no way I could safely cross the path in complete darkness.

I knew I was fatigued and now realized we were possibly in danger of dying. I was getting physically exhausted, and I needed to stay focused on every step and every movement. I thought about my daughters.

"Get your F-ing ass home!" I yelled at the top of my lungs.

Twenty minutes later, we reached what we believed to be the summit of Mt. Hood. Usually, at this point, we would hug it out, high five one another, and celebrate the accomplishment. Instead, we were focused on trying to find a safe exit off of the mountain. Despite thirty minutes of searching in whiteout conditions in the dark, we couldn't find a safe way down. Someone was going to get hurt or possibly worse if we took the chance.

Finally, we huddled together.

Unable to hear one another even from close range, I yelled, "We're going to have to dig a hole!"

Nobody wanted to admit to it, but Keith yelled back, "He's right."

For the next three hours, we dug into the ice with ice axes and one shovel. After fourteen hours of continuous stressful climbing, we were spent, but working on the cave was the only way to keep warm. The estimated wind chill was forty below, and we needed shelter quickly.

Around 9:00 p.m., we finished carving a small but claustrophobic hole for the five of us. As I stated, the low snowfall up to that point in the year made it difficult to dig an adequately sized snow cave, and as we climbed into our bivouac sacks, we found ourselves with very little space between us and the roof of the cave.

However, we were finally out of the vicious storm, and I immediately noticed the silence within the cave. We didn't speak for a while as each of us tried to find a comfortable position within the cramped hole to get warm. All of us were dehydrated, exhausted, and frozen—no water and no stove (which was a huge mistake on our part). Without saying anything, we knew we were in for a long, tough night.

Then suddenly, about an hour later, I heard Jim moaning next to me. He was a big man, a hard man with big hands, a construction worker. He was cold and hypothermic. His body was shaking and shivering uncontrollably, so I instantly tried wrapping my body around his in an effort to warm him. Keep in mind, in these circumstances, one does whatever it takes to stay alive, and none of us was concerned about any type of "man code."

Finally, Jim's shivering subsided, but his breathing was worrisome. The last thing we wanted to do despite the situation was call for a rescue. Jim was in training for the local mountain rescue team, and we figured that we got ourselves into this predicament, so it was up to us to ride out the night and hope the storm diminished by morning. But after thirty minutes of listening to Jim's breaths, we made the 911 call from the cave.

David spoke to the sheriff's office and shared our situation. He said that one of our team members was hypothermic and we were doing our best to get him warm. He also said we were going to try to ride out the night and find a way down in the morning. The sheriff asked for us to stay put and reconnect in the early morning as there was no possibility of sending a rescue team up high on the mountain in the conditions we were facing. We agreed.

About an hour after the call, I had my own shivering attack. My body was so cold that I could feel my bones when I moved and shuffled myself for comfort. Unexpectedly, my legs started kicking uncontrollably for about forty-five seconds. It was a painful experience that would occur four or five times through the night.

Water was now dripping from the roof of the cave from condensation and freezing instantly onto our bivouac sacks and clothes. Sleep was not an option. As soon as I would nod off, my body would awake with violent shivers. Time was moving fast and slow all at the same time.

Hours into the night, I then heard David say, "Guys, we need to remain calm and come up with a quick plan. The hole of the cave is filled in, and we're going to suffocate if we don't keep our shit together."

It was 3:00 a.m., and after twenty-fours without water, climbing through a relentless storm to 11,000 feet bringing fifty mph winds including minus forty-degree wind chills—as well as hours building a pathetic snow shelter near the summit of the mountain—the fear inside of me was now at its peak. I looked down at my feet, searching for the hole of the pit, and sure enough, it was gone.

There was no way out. We were possibly going to die inside that hole on top of Mt. Hood if we didn't do something quickly.

We did stay calm and methodical. There wasn't much room to move, but it was decided that I had the best position to kick us out. It took a lot of careful maneuvering, and eventually, I got into a place to give me leverage to kick. I laid down on my chest into the snow and began kicking like a donkey in an effort to unbury ourselves. My face was stuck in the snow and ice as I kicked and kicked. My heart was racing as I feared suffocation, and finally, I hit air and crawled out into the storm. Immediately, I began digging out a trench in front of the cave. All of our gear was buried, and I had to jump back into the cave to get out of the elements.

The storm remained violent.

I was covered in ice when I came back into the cave, and Bob instantly spooned me to get me warm. The shivering started once again. When I recovered, I remembered, "Embrace the suffering. It's what you signed up for." I put that quote on repeat within my mind.

A couple of hours later, as the darkness lifted, the sheriff called us and stated that a rescue team was headed up. We even received a call from The Brominator. He was part of the mountain rescue team and directed us to stay put.

By this time, Broms had become a really good friend of mine, not just a climbing partner, and the conversation ended emotionally.

"You guys hang in there, Jarod." I could tell he was a little choked up.

He knew we were in a bad situation. Later, after joining the rescue team myself, I found out that there were arguments on whether or not it was safe to execute an attempt to get us off the mountain.

Soon after, Bob volunteered to ensure that the entry to the cave was safe and did his best to unbury our backpacks and gear. After a period of time, he started yelling into the cave that he thought he had seen someone on the mountain looking for us. I believed him and came out for a quick look, but realized he was hallucinating. The clouds were swirling and creating ghost-like figures.

After Bob returned to the cave, a few hours went by. More shivering. More concern on whether or not we were going to make it out alive. Finally, the sheriff called and said that the rescue team was on their way up, but the conditions were slowing them down.

We were directed to stay put, but I told the guys, "If we stay in this cave, one of us isn't going to make it through the night. I say we wait until noon, and if nobody is here, we grab our gear and find a way to get our asses down."

The team agreed, and we waited. Our bones were frozen. It took the breath out of us to simply move into a "comfortable" position. And as the clock kept ticking, I thought to myself that it was impossible for the rescue team to get to us safely. They were putting their own lives on the line.

I couldn't wait any longer. It was 11:30 a.m. We'd spent fourteen-and-a-half hours in the cave, nearly thirty-two hours without water or food. I crawled out of the cave and started digging for our packs and gear. The storm continued to rage, and I could see those imaginary people that Bob saw through the clouds as well.

Then suddenly, I saw a red jacket pop up over the cliff in front of me! Then another. One of the rescue team members was Marty J. He and I had climbed Dragontail Peak in Washington state the year before.

"Are all you guys mobile?" he yelled.

I said, "Yes!"

"Then let's get your shit and get the F out of here!"

And we did—cautiously. High winds and two feet of fresh snow were a prime recipe for an avalanche. (We later found out that one of the rescuers did indeed get caught in a slide on his way up to us.) The downclimbing was sketchy, visibility was still low, and the south side of the mountain seemed foreign, although I had climbed it so many times before.

Finally, at 8,500 feet, we were safe and placed in a snowcat. On the ride down, we were warned that the national news media was covering our situation and wanted a press conference with all of us to explain what happened. A couple of the guys said that they weren't going to speak, but I reminded them that there were probably quite a few people that helped get us down safely, some risking their lives to do so.

"F pride. We need to share our lessons learned."

Eventually, we reached Timberline Lodge, and when it was my turn to exit the snowcat, The Brominator was right there. We hugged it out.

The rescue team and EMTs were also amazing. They gave us warm drinks, dry coats, some food, and checked us out for any injuries. I could feel my hands and feet thawing, particularly my ring finger.

We then sat down for a press conference, and we were all surprised at the number of cameras and microphones. It must have been a slow news day because apparently our situation was a big deal.

On the ride home, the pain in my fingers began to worsen, and my ring finger began to puff up as my wedding band was cutting off circulation. I immediately went to the ER. After cutting my ring off, the doctor stated that I had bad frostbite and was going to need to see a specialist quickly.

For two months, I couldn't button my shirts or tie my shoes, and at one point, the doc told me that he was going to have cut digits from three of my fingers. Jim lost part of his thumb, but I was lucky as my physical therapist held me accountable with multiple ultrasound treatments on a weekly basis to re-stimulate the nerves.

Days after the event, following a doctor's appointment, I pulled over to the side of the freeway. My fingers were black. I had to wear slippers until my feet healed up, as my toes were also frostbitten. I realized then and there how lucky I was. I was back home safe with my two beautiful daughters. They were my main motivation to keep pushing myself that day and have always been my main reason for never giving up, no matter what challenge has been in front of me.

I sobbed for a long time on the side of that freeway.

And I was grateful for the lessons learned. I shared our experience with local climbing groups, as well as my frostbite doc's school of juvenile students (in exchange for his medical services, he asked me to do so).

My lessons?

Humility

The mountain humbled me. The mountains and Mother Nature are powerful and must be respected. Expect the best, but plan for the worst. We didn't do that. No stove meant no water and no warmth. And yes, I've been in whiteout conditions since those two days on Mt. Hood, but I do everything to avoid bad weather. In fact, I now constantly look behind me for clouds, no matter what the forecast says.

We're stronger than we think

A woman at one of my speaking engagements came up to me after the event and stated, "I don't think I could have survived that situation."

I responded, "Yes, you could. You don't know what you really have deep inside of you until you're fighting for your life. You become an animal and will do whatever it takes to survive."

Please note that there was nothing heroic about my story of survival. It was a choice followed by a lot of other bad choices that could have been avoided, but I do believe we all possess an animalistic spirit within us.

Diligence

Our climb was filled with chaos, uncertainty, and fear. We couldn't hear at times, nor did we have visibility, but we all have to continue the fight and ward off carelessness, as well as laziness. Stay present. Be aware of the moment. Do the work. Dig that hole if it's going to save your life, no matter how hard it is.

One other thing: Take care of your team. Do whatever it takes to keep them safe.

And last, but not least...

I realized after our Mt. Hood fiasco that I was selfish. Yes, I was and continue to be passionate about climbing and the mountains. They fuel my spirit, no doubt. However, to die on the mountain wouldn't be fair to my children or my friends. I've lost some of my best friends because of their adventures, and there will always be a painful void in my life and their families' lives without them here today.

I couldn't imagine leaving this gift of life because of my own selfish pursuits. I climb and ride to laugh, live to the fullest, regain lost confidence, and see things that many don't get the opportunity to see. But there is no honor in dying in the mountains. In many ways, life is like a climb, full of obstacles and challenges. And just like life, we must develop the resilience and discipline to do what is necessary, as well as accomplish big goals.

But we never, ever quit. We *keep climbing.*

About Jarod Cogswell

Jarod Cogswell is the co-creator and Director of Sport and Education for DEKA (Spartan Race), the founder of WORK Like an Athlete fitness business consulting services, a Todd Durkin mastermind platinum-level business coach, gym owner, Alpha Warrior U.S. Army BOSS Strong Coach, twenty-five-year fitness industry leader, keynote speaker, high-energy performance enhancement coach, and author.

Jarod is a passionate mountain athlete, ski mountaineer, former Portland Mountain Rescue team member, and proud father of two daughters.

JAROD COGSWELL

- Leadership Training

- Culture Enhancement

- Sales and Service Training

- Financial Performance

- Marketing and Branding

- Fitness Programming

- Keynote Speaking

Phone: 971.998.7312

Website: http://worklikeanathlete.com/

CHAPTER 10

Prayer Over Fear

by Theresa Poston

We all face fear at some point in our lives. Some people face fear many times throughout their lives, and the fears come in different sizes. Our fears are shaped differently. We could have a fear of trying a new experience, a fear of heights, of wild animals, or of crossing a busy street. And then there are fears of loss, loneliness, or illness. Maybe some of us face fear all the time.

When one fear ends, a new one begins. But I know that we aren't made to fear. We are made to have faith, hope, and strength to face our fears. These attributes come from a relationship with Jesus Christ. Psalms 34:4 tells us, "I sought the Lord, and he answered me; he delivered me from all my fear." But how do we get access to this? Through hitting the floor on our knees and opening the Bible—we pray.

There is a verse In the Bible that has been my life verse for the last fifteen years or more; Romans 8:28: "And we know that in all things God works for the good of those who love Him, who have been called according to his purpose." This verse doesn't specifically tell us not to fear, but to me, it means that everything I experience is to fulfill God's purpose, and because I love Him, it will be okay, and I am not to be afraid. This seems simple enough to me, but right now and for the last seven weeks, it hasn't been as easy as I thought.

I recently found out that I may have a frightening health issue. Since then, I've had a sonogram and an MRI. I was then sent for an upper GI endoscopy with fine-needle aspiration of a tumor on my stomach lining. Maybe some people wouldn't be afraid until more is known, but I was absolutely fearful—horrified, actually. I was afraid of the unknown results, and I was afraid of the procedure, too. My husband Bob and I talked about the possibilities, and the look of fear in Bob's eyes when we talked about it reflected my own fear. I couldn't stop thinking about what would happen to him, our adult children, and grandchildren. My inward struggle with my fear, my deep personal fear of illness, is almost too much for me to even speak of.

But if I'm a Christian woman, how can I be afraid? Is it not shameful for me to be so faithless? Is it not a sin? I wrestled with these thoughts during the day, and they kept me awake at night too. This was an intense emotional and spiritual battle for me, but what could I do at this point? I prayed. And I know that I am blessed by all the prayers being said for me.

I'm not a stranger to prayer, and my belief in the power it possesses is certainly tangible. I have experienced answered prayers in the past, and I have seen my prayers for others answered too. I have prayed for direction about important decisions I needed to make about relationships, healing from illness, and spiritual and emotional brokenness, and I have even prayed about day-to-day tasks. I pray many times throughout the day, no matter where I am or what I'm doing. Over the years, I have learned to first turn to prayer for advice and not to friends or family members. Oh, I still talk about situations with them, but prayer is my first response to life situations. My prayers are often simple but honest conversations with God because this is the relationship I have with Him. Sometimes the answers aren't what I've prayed for, but the outcome always proves to be the best for the situation.

During this particular health scare I was going through, my husband has asked family and friends to pray for me, and I have asked for prayers, too. Soon after we started asking for prayers, on a morning at work, I suddenly felt a strong wave of peace washing over me. I am certain I was feeling prayers from others. I have had this feeling several times since then that gives me a break from the exhausting worry and fear, and it gives me a great burst of energy to know that others are praying on my behalf. I believe God is using these feelings to bolster my faith and perseverance. He is letting me know that He is in control and working every moment on my behalf, and I am not to be afraid. I may not be settled in peace at every moment, but I know that prayer works, I know that God has a good plan for me, I know the Bible is His Word for comfort and wisdom.

I had my upper GI endoscopy, but tumor aspiration wasn't performed because there was no tumor! Over the weeks, several doctors looked at the tumor on the MRI images and advised me what to do, but now there is no tumor there. I know this is God. I know my prayers and everyone else's prayers were not for nothing. I am blessed and so grateful.

Psalms 30:2 says, "O Lord my God, I called to you for help and you healed me." I will continue to pray about my health, as I will have a CT scan performed in six months to see if a tumor is still not there. I also am less fearful because this has assured me that fear can also be conquered with prayer.

I know God places difficulties in our lives in order for us to glorify Him as we work to overcome them. And difficult times are used by God to draw us into a closer relationship with Him. I imagine that when I get through this time, my worries will have been for nothing because I'll be healed. But I also imagine that my life will change, and I'll need to change how I live day to day. Either way, God has provided me with the power to face each day, and He will continue to provide me with this power in the days ahead.

There will be days when it will be hard to remember this, and there will be days when I will feel such peace that I know I don't have to be afraid because He is my strength and He has a good plan for me. It's only been a few weeks, but I know this experience is teaching me to draw nearer to God to know His presence, His strength, and His power. It is teaching me that dropping to my knees in prayer and opening my Bible is so powerful and miraculous. After all, the same spirit that raised Christ dwells inside me. His goodness is here now and will be there tomorrow.

About Theresa Poston

Theresa Poston is a Christian, a retired federal government employee, wife, mother of two adult children, and she has five wonderful grandchildren. She enjoys spending time with her family, traveling, being outdoors, and photography. She also likes to read a good book, fiction and non-fiction, from time to time. Theresa is a lover of animals and supports animal adoption instead of breeding them. She was born and raised in Virginia and moved with her husband and children to Maryland, where she currently lives.